The Client's Bible

The Client's Bible

How to select, manage, and get
maximum value from your
advertising agency

Stanley Newhoff

Firefish
PUBLISHING COMPANY

Firefish Publishing Company

ISBN 978-0615439495

Introduction

A man walked into his doctor's office, announced that he had a mild case of sciatica, prescribed an anti-inflammatory and a muscle relaxant, and informed the doctor that he needed these prescriptions by 4:00 PM the same day.

Not a likely scenario.

Yet advertising clients routinely self-diagnose their own marketing ailment, prescribe the remedy, and give their advertising agency an unrealistic deadline to do something that may not actually solve the problem. This is not because they are bad people. It's because they really don't understand what agencies do—and vastly underestimate what a good agency can do for them.

A good agency is a cooperative association of highly trained marketing experts and creative artists who are in the business of helping clients succeed. A successful relationship with such a group is one of partnership and mutual respect.

The key ingredients are collaboration, open dialogue, active listening on both sides of the table, and willingness to explore new ideas on every level.

This book is intended to show you how to select and work with your agency so you can enjoy the full benefit of their skill and expertise—and take better results to the bank.

Chapter 1

How to Select an Agency

Don't Call In The Cows

A cattle call may deliver only cows. Do your homework and interview a select group of qualified agencies. If you live in a specialized world—heart valves, political advertising, petroleum processing, military supercomputers—talk to agencies that have at least some experience in your field or a related field.

It is not really necessary for a prospective agency to have direct experience in your specific specialty. For example, an agency with extensive experience in marketing heart valves would probably do a great job marketing your angioplasty catheter. But an agency that has never done work in the medical field would probably not be your best choice.

In the real world, most agencies that specialize in certain kinds of marketing were started by people who became experts in that market while working for another agency. They worked under the supervision and tutelage of experts and gradually developed their own understanding and expertise as they gained first-hand experience. This happens over a period of years, not weeks or months. This expertise is valuable. Your best bet is to find such an agency and treasure them.

1

The Agency Search

Provide each agency with written questions at least three weeks before the initial meeting. Depending upon your specific interests, these questions may include the following:

- How long has your agency been in business?
- Who are your current clients?
- What 3 references can we contact for follow-up?
- What experience does your agency have in our sector or a related sector? Please provide case studies.
- What is your agency's history?
- What is your agency's philosophy?
- What are your agency's core capabilities?
- How does your agency differentiate itself from competitive agencies?
- With what clients have you had long-term relationships (more than 5 years)? How and why has each been successful?
- Do you currently work with any client(s) who may pose a conflict in managing our account?
- What would be the structure of the team assigned to our account? How would resources be allocated?
- What specific team members would work on our account? Please provide bios.
- What resources do you have to manage periods of high demand?
- Who would be responsible for managing the day-to-day relationship, including timelines and budgets?

Allow each agency to present their credentials and answer your questions in person at the initial meeting. Make sure that all decision-makers from your company attend this meeting and stay for the entire meeting.

Also make sure that the actual agency team you will be working with are at this initial meeting. This should consist of the Account Executive who will handle your account on a day-to-day basis and the lead Copywriter and Art Director. There may also be agency brass at the meeting and they may want to meet with you first, but insist on meeting your team. It is unlikely the brass will be doing any of the strategic or creative work and you have to get a sense of the people you will be working with.

From this round of initial meetings, select the agencies that seem qualified to work on your account and who also seem like the sort of people your team would like to work with. Do not underestimate the importance of chemistry in selecting and working with an agency. Ideally, it is a collaborative partnership. To be successful, it will require a common base of knowledge and mutual respect—and a good deal of personal compatibility.

Select a short list of agencies you think you'd like to work with and meet with them a second time. Give each agency the same marketing and creative assignment. Brief each agency on your company and as much marketing information as you can safely reveal. (See Chapter 3 for a guide to creative input.) Make sure the creative team is at the briefing session—the work will be better and it establishes the right working dynamic. Set a specific time for presentation of a brief marketing approach and associated creative ideas based on your input and allow enough time for the agency to do a good job. At least two weeks is minimal, more if you can afford to wait.

The Agency Presentation

Make sure all decision-makers and influencers are at the meeting when the agency presents their marketing and creative solution(s) for the assignment you gave them. Set aside a sufficient block of time (at least 2 hours). Turn off all cell phones, give instructions that the meeting is not to be interrupted for any reason, and give each agency your undivided, unhurried attention. Make sure everyone who is to attend the meeting is there at the beginning and stays for the entire presentation. Ideally, this will be the same group that attended the initial presentation. Do not let the President "drop in" for a while and then disappear. It is impossible to make an intelligent presentation with people coming and going. It is also extremely rude. If any decision-maker cannot make the meeting, reschedule it.

Pay attention to each agency's reasoning as well as the creative solution(s). You must judge whether they hit the mark BASED ON THE INFORMATION YOU GAVE THEM AND THE ADDITIONAL INFORMATION THEY WERE ABLE TO FIND THROUGH THEIR OWN RESEARCH. You will always know more than the agency about your product and your market. They can't read your mind. They can only work with the information they have.

Evaluating Strategic Thinking

Make sure you evaluate the strength of the agency's strategic thinking as well as the power of the creative work.

- Do they understand your market?
- Do they understand your customers?
- Do they recognize the strengths and weaknesses of your competitors?
- Have they differentiated your product or service in a meaningful way?
- Have they gone beyond the obvious in framing your key selling messages?
- Have they identified the key purchasing decision factors?
- Have they "nailed it" in presenting your core competitive advantages?

Evaluating Creative

Evaluating creative work can be tricky because it is an art form, and therefore essentially subjective. It is easy to be seduced by beautiful graphics and clever headlines. However, professional creative work must be held responsible for helping to achieve specific marketing objectives and should be judged accordingly.

- Does each concept present a single, clear idea that promotes a specific marketing message?
- Are the messages consistent with the agency's strategic presentation?
- Does the headline and image in each concept work together to present a cohesive message? (Hint: if either the

headline or image works by itself, it's not a cohesive message.)

- Does the overall impression of the creative work fit with the positioning and branding suggested in the strategic presentation?
- Is the creative work appropriate for the marketplace? (Surfers and doctors respond to different marketing styles.)
- Is there a clear call to action?
- Does the primary message offer a compelling reason to take the action requested?

Agency Selection

As soon as all agencies have presented their work, gather the team of decision-makers and make a decision. Do not prolong this process. The sooner you make a decision, the better. This meeting should be run by a strong facilitator—ideally the marketing person who will be the agency's primary contact.

Before the group engages in endless debate, the facilitator should have each decision-maker independently rank the agencies in order of preference on a piece of paper that contains only the names of the agencies and not the name of the decision-maker. The results should then be tallied in front of the group on a white board. It is important that this occur before the CEO or any other 800-pound gorilla has an opportunity to influence the group and short-circuit their individual instincts. Debate will inevitably ensue thereafter, but at least an objective vote will have been taken and this should be used as a benchmark of the group's collective wisdom.

Notifying the Winning Agency

As soon as you have selected an agency, have your CEO call their CEO to congratulate him/her and the agency team that made the winning presentation. You may even send over champagne or a box of fruit as a friendly gesture. Follow up with a formal letter appointing the agency and arrange for whatever paperwork is required by your company and/or the agency. Then schedule a meeting with the agency Account Executive and, if appropriate, the creative team to provide input on the first planning or creative project.

All of those gestures of respect and enthusiasm will pay big dividends as you begin to work with your agency team.

Notifying the Other Agencies

On the same day that you notify the winning agency, send a personal note to the other agency finalists thanking them for the effort they put into their presentation and the quality of their work. Let them know that it was a difficult decision (which it typically is) and that you will keep them in mind if the situation changes.

This accomplishes two things. First, it is the proper thing to do. Second, it keeps the door open in case the winning agency doesn't work out for you.

It is important to notify all of the finalists who did not win at the same time that you notify the winning agency so they hear it from you and not from a media rep, the grapevine, or the news release published by the winning agency.

Chapter 2

How to Work With an Agency

Respect

Treat your agency people like partners, not like vendors. They are usually talented, experienced, and passionate about their work. They know more than you do about their individual specialties and can add enormous value to your marketing planning, creative strategy, and the success of your brands.

Your agency team typically gets personally invested in helping you succeed. They work hard at understanding your corporate culture, the personality of your various brands, the strengths and weaknesses of your brands and competitive brands, and the technology behind your products. Talk to them. Listen to them. Let them in on the information they need to help you.

> **Tell me**
> **and I will want to resist.**
> **Ask me**
> **and I will want to help.**

Above all, do not dictate from on high as though your agency is just the hired help. The relationships will sour. The work will suffer. And eventually the agency will go away.

It's only human nature.

Non-disclosure Agreements

In order to work collaboratively with your agency, you will have to provide information you would not like to share with your competitors. So it makes sense to have the agency execute a formal non-disclosure agreement. Your legal counsel can draw one up if you don't already have one, or you can download one from the Web. You may only have the agency executives sign the agreement or require that every employee of the agency who may come into contact with your information also sign it. Check with your legal counsel to decide.

Collaboration

Your agency team often becomes an advocacy group for you. They want to know all about your company and your products and *they want to be involved* in helping you succeed. The more you can let them know what's going on in your company, why decisions are being made, and what's going on in your marketplace, the more they can help you—and the more they will want to. It's OK to ask your agency questions about market threats and opportunities, possible strategies, and potential line extensions or new products. You don't have to follow their advice, but you may be surprised how helpful it can be.

Invite them to your company for strategic brainstorming sessions with each of your key brand managers, take notes on big notepads, and spread those big note pages all over the walls. Have those notes transcribed and send the document to the agency, add your day-after insights, and ask the agency for their additional insights. Six or 12 months later, have each of your brand managers go to the agency and do the same thing all over again. You will be amazed at the valuable insights that come out of this simple exercise.

As one of my clients often says, companies tend to "drink their own Kool-Aid." Sharing the planning with your agency will help to make it more objective.

> **Companies tend to**
> **"drink their own Kool-Aid."**
> **Your agency can help**
> **you stay objective.**

Input

Computer specialists have a simple formula that aptly describes the results of bad input. They call the phenomenon GIGO: Garbage In, Garbage Out. The same formula applies to creative input. Your account and creative teams can only base their work on what you tell them. They will usually do a little research on their own to better understand your company, your brands, your industry, and your competitors, But for each specific creative assignment, they will rely on you to provide critical guidance.

What they need is not all that complicated. It's all in the Creative Input Form.

The Creative Input Form

Most agencies have a formal document called the *Creative Input Form* or *Creative Brief* or something similar. One way or another, they try to formalize the input given to the creative team for every project. This is important. It saves time and money and produces better work.

Chapter 3 gives you a guided tour of the typical Creative Input Form and what kind of information is required for each section. You need to take this process seriously. The more you help your agency get this right, the more efficiently they can help you achieve your marketing objectives.

Chapter 3

The Creative Input Form: A User's Manual

Clear and comprehensive input is the raw material out of which great creative work is made. The better the input, the better and more cost-effective the work is likely to be. Here's a brief guide for using the Creative Input Form effectively. The headings below, or variations of them, are typical sections in the input form most agencies use.

Target Audience:

This should be divided into *Primary Audience, Secondary Audience,* and *Tertiary Audience.* You can't really talk to everyone simultaneously and say anything compelling.

Communications Objective:

This is an important factor. It's not "buy the product," although that's typically the ultimate reason companies run advertising. But advertising does not sell product unless it is direct response advertising. The kind of advertising most agencies do **creates a favorable selling climate** for a product. It is up to the sales rep to close the sale or the customer to go to the supplier or website where the product is available and make a purchase. The real question here is: **What must this communications vehicle accomplish?**

This is a key insight for the creative team into the primary marketing purpose of this creative communications vehicle. The communications objective is *an execution of a marketing strategy*. For example, do we want to:

- Reverse a negative impression of the product?
- Neutralize a competitive threat?
- Reinforce the product's Unique Selling Proposition (USP) or Brand Promise?
- Bolster credibility?
- Emphasize a new indication for a medical product?
- Change audience perceptions?
- Educate the audience about something important?
- Increase awareness of the brand, product, or company?

Call to Action:

This should tell the creative team exactly what we want to reader/viewer to do. Again, it's not always "buy the product." It's a *specific action intended to pave the way for a sale*. For example:

- Call your sales representative for more information
- Fill out the business reply card (BRC)
- Ask your retailer/doctor about it
- Visit our website
- Visit our convention booth
- Call the 800 number
- Prescribe this product (if you're a doctor)

- Go to the store and buy it (if you're a consumer)

Reason Why (Primary Message):

This is the single most compelling reason the audience should take the action we want (the Call to Action). It's not a list of reasons, or a table of features and benefits. *It's the single most compelling reason.* Typically it's a major benefit to the customer. Examples include:

- The embarrassment of facial pimples will be gone in two days
- All the men on the beach will admire your trim body
- Your boss will be pleased that you have mastered this computer program
- This easy-to-implant heart valve will allow you to get your patients off the heart/lung machine faster

To be really effective, an ad or other communications vehicle can have only one primary message, delivered with totally integrated visual and verbal components (i.e., the primary graphic and headline).

**Cardinal rule of advertising:
"One ad, one point."**

Special Considerations:

This is a hidden goldmine. Rather than focusing only on logistical issues like delivery instructions and accelerated schedules (typically handled in separate status reports and timelines anyway), it's far more useful to provide information about competitive issues, market dynamics, regulatory problems, product recalls, product failures, impending launches of new and superior competitive products, etc. The creative team will be helped a great deal knowing that the primary competitor's sales reps are out there right now telling the docs that our client's new angioplasty balloon tends to explode as soon as it's introduced into the patient. And that it's not true.

Features and Benefits:

It's helpful to have a list of features and their associated benefits. A feature without a benefit is useless for creative development. The prospective customer does not care why the client likes the product or how well it is designed. The customer is only interested in how it makes his/her life easier, more pleasant, or more profitable—and how it solves *significant problems*.

> **A great product
> that solves trivial problems
> will be perceived
> as a trivial product.**

Competitive Products:

It's good to know who the enemies are—and how they compare with our product.

Competitive Advantages:

How do we outgun our competition? What unique value does this product bring to the market? Why should anyone care?

Competitive Disadvantages

How are we outgunned by the competition? Where are we vulnerable? What can we say to a prospective customer to minimize these disadvantages?

Chapter 4

Nurturing The Relationship

Decision-Making

A story is told about one of David Ogilvy's classic moments with a prospective new client. David showed up for a new business presentation and was shown to a large conference room with approximately 20 people sitting around the table. The person facilitating the meeting explained that David would have 30 minutes to make his presentation, after which the facilitator would ring a bell and David would be required to stop whether or not he had completed the presentation.

David looked at the people sitting around the table and then spoke to the facilitator, "Before I begin," he said "tell me...how many of these people will be involved in reviewing the agency's creative work"?

"Why, all of them," replied the facilitator.

David hesitated for a second, and then said, "Ring the bell."

The creative process is a fragile and subjective series of inspirations woven together into a cohesive and compelling fabric. Great creative moves us on many levels and touches our hearts as well as our minds. You cannot dissect this complex tapestry like a crazy quilt and interchange parts from another pattern. Your ideas

18

may be great on their own, but totally inappropriate if inserted into a different conceptual framework.

> **The ideas of a half-dozen people can't be imposed on an organic work of art without killing it.**

The answer is to appoint a single person to provide feedback to the agency after everybody inside your company has given their feedback to that person. That person needs to assess the feedback, decide what is and is not appropriate, and transmit the appropriate information in an organized fashion to the agency all at once. This does NOT mean rewriting and redesigning the work. It means communicating legitimate concerns ABOUT specific aspects of the work and necessary corrections for accuracy and legality. It must be left to the agency to figure out how to accommodate those concerns and corrections on the next version.

One of the most successful how-to books I ever wrote was commissioned by a paint manufacturer to be distributed to their customers. My agency presented the manuscript to the President for his feedback. After he reviewed it, he circulated the manuscript to various experts inside his company with the following instructions:

> *"Please review this manuscript for accuracy and content. Comments on style are not necessary. I like it the way it is."*

As a result of his leadership, the feedback we received was pertinent, factual, and extremely helpful in getting the right information to the consumer. No time was wasted arm-wrestling over commas, dependent clauses, or tone. The book was extremely successful in promoting the company's product because it was not written by engineers for engineers. It was written by a professional writer for normal people, with a light-hearted tone and tons of directly useful information that was easy to understand.

Planning

For a partnership between a client and an agency to work, there must be one person in each organization with responsibility AND AUTHORITY to conduct the business of the partnership. Committees generate garbage. You cannot develop incisive marketing strategy or powerful creative work by committee. Committees arrive at conclusions by consensus. Consensus is not brilliance, it is compromise. Winning in the marketing arena requires brilliance. Only talented individuals working in small teams approach brilliance. A talented Marketing Manager working with a talented Account Executive can develop marketing plans and strategies that will knock your socks off. A committee containing the same people but weighed down with the opinions and prejudices of other people will typically produce plans that have all the appeal of a wet sock.

Your Best Friend—The Account Executive

Agency Account Executives are notorious for adopting their clients and advocating for them. Your Account Executive is your best friend in the Agency and the very best tool you have for getting what you need when you need it for a price you can afford.

To take full advantage of the dedication and skill of your Account Executive, you need to tell him/her the truth and treat him/her as a valued member of your marketing team—which (s)he is.

- Include your Account Executive in advance planning
- Copy him/her on competitive press and relevant articles
- Share your short- and long-term marketing plans and product introductions
- Share market dynamics, competitive threats, relevant industry trends
- Seek your Account Executive's input on handling marketing threats and exploiting opportunities
- Collaborate with your Account Executive on developing your marketing plan, monitoring progress, and making mid-course corrections
- Work with your Account Executive to develop a single-minded marketing purpose for each communications vehicle

Your Account Executive has a delicate task to perform. (S)he must represent you inside the Agency and represent the Agency to you. It is not useful or appropriate to consider any aspect of this relationship as adversarial. It should all be collegial, open, and collaborative. The Account Executive wants to deliver marketing planning and materials to you that fit with your corporate culture and produce dramatic results, the creative team wants to develop strong and effective marketing materials that will ring the cash register, and you want your company to succeed beyond the CEO's wildest dreams. Those desires and objectives can all be best achieved by working together as a team and not as warring factions.

The Care and Feeding of Your Creative Team

As previously mentioned, your creative team wants to produce great work and help your company dominate your industry sector. They are highly trained, sensitive, and dedicated artists who take pride in their work. Working effectively with them requires a bit of delicacy on your part. Here are some useful guidelines.

Do not design ads or write copy. You are not qualified. If you are as good as your creative team, fire your agency. If you are not as good as your creative team, get out of the way and let them do what they're trained to do. Creative people work very hard to perfect their work. They are passionate, dedicated, and extremely proud of what they do. If you mess with their work, they will no longer be able to be as passionate, dedicated, or proud. It's basic human nature. You will demotivate them to the point where they will try to give you what they think you want just to avoid the pain of having you continually violate their offspring. You will no longer get their best work. You will get your own prejudices reflected back at you.

The proper way to change creative work is to explain very clearly to the creative team directly, not through the Account Executive, exactly what is wrong, inaccurate, or just plain inappropriate in the current work and ask them to fix it. The more information you give the creative team, and the more explicitly you explain the problem, the more quickly and effectively they will be able to develop a better creative concept or execution.

The best Marketing Directors never bring a pencil to a meeting with the creative team. They never write on the work. They never suggest new wording or new pictures. They never argue over the placement of commas or the color of the background. They simply explain where it hurts and let the doctor diagnose and recommend a cure. They also get the most enthusiastic cooperation and devotion from their creative teams and the best creative work. You do the math.

It is important to note that the agency Account Executive should also resist the temptation to edit, revise, or otherwise mess with the creative work before, during, or after presenting it to the client. Nothing should ever be changed on creative work by anyone except the creative team. Period. It may take some discussion, some explanation, some arm-twisting, but the more consistently you go to the creative team for changes rather than making arbitrary changes yourself, the more willing cooperation you will experience. You may even discover once in awhile after talking through your rationale with the creative team that the change you wanted to make is not such a good idea, after all—or that there is a better way to achieve your objective.

A Case In Point

Consider this scenario. You are the client Marketing Director. You have spent two weeks collaborating with the agency Account Executive on a marketing plan to be presented to the Board of Directors. You have worked very hard on this plan. After analyzing the research, considering all relevant market forces, and doing a little primary research of your own, you and the agency Account Executive feel really good about your conclusions, the associated strategies, and the recommended tactics for implementing those strategies. You are very proud of your work on this plan and relish the opportunity to share it with the Board. Two days before presentation to the Board, you give the plan to your boss, the VP of Marketing and Sales, for a final review.

You do not get any immediate feedback, but on the morning of the Board meeting, a copy of the plan shows up on your desk with a note from your boss indicating that advance copies have been sent to the Board for their review and he looks forward to the discussion with the Board that afternoon. You open the report and read through it in order to savor what you expect will be a rich discussion with the Board about the innovative and insightful ideas you and the agency Account Executive came up with. But you discover that the plan has been almost entirely rewritten, your best ideas have been removed, and it is now a standard, predictable, and very superficial rehash of the same old crap the company has been doing for the past decade. How do you feel now? Do you look forward to the Board meeting? Are you excited about working that hard for your boss next time? Are you grateful that his "review" made the plan better? Of course not. You'd like to kill the sonofabitch very slowly with a small, dull pocketknife.

Now imagine that marketing plan is an ad and you are part of the creative team that sweated bullets making it as good as it could be before the client arbitrarily changed it.

Chapter 5

How To Evaluate Creative Work

Giving Feedback

As mentioned earlier, do not rewrite copy or redesign layouts. Do not prescribe solutions. Identify problems or errors and let the agency come back to you with solutions. Do not diagnose your own disease and prescribe a cure. Tell the doctor where it hurts and get a professional recommendation for an appropriate remedy. This approach will not only produce better advertising, it will produce a healthier and more successful relationship with your agency.

How to Proceed

Start every discussion explaining what you LIKE about the work. Don't start off looking for problems.

Now provide the creative team with an objective analysis based on the marketing objectives. Is it on target? Does it communicate the appropriate marketing messages? If so, do not be quick to reject the creative executions just because they are not what you expected. They may be better than you expected. Be open to new ways of communicating—what you have done before or what your competitors are doing may not be the best thing you can do. If they do **NOT** communicate the appropriate marketing messages, talk about the marketing situation, the competition, the purpose of the marketing vehicle, the specific strategic objectives

26

of the piece, the competitive advantages of the product or service, the needs and perceptions of the audience, and other relevant issues. Then give the agency enough time to revise the work intelligently.

When they present the revised work, start the discussion by reviewing the previous version and revisiting your comments and concerns. That will establish the target the new work is supposed to be shooting for. Again, describe what's right with it and then carefully evaluate how well it achieves the marketing objectives. If it's on target but still makes you a little uncomfortable, that may be a signal that it's strong enough to be wildly effective in the marketplace.

If the work is still off-target or somehow inappropriate, repeat the discussion of the marketing situation, the competition, the purpose of the marketing vehicle, the specific strategic objectives of the piece, the competitive advantages of the product or service, the needs and perceptions of the audience, and other relevant issues. Give the Agency another week or so to revise the work. If it's still off-target or unacceptable a second time, it may be a signal that it's time to look for another Agency.

True Concept

The strongest creative is the *True Concept*. The *True Concept* consists of a visual and headline that work together to create meaning in the viewer's mind. A decorated headline is not a True Concept and is not as powerful.

What is a true concept?

- Total integration of headline and visual
- Presents a single, cohesive message
- Neither headline nor visual tells the whole story—both are needed
- The meaning is created in the mind of the reader / viewer by combining the headline and visual

Example of a True Concept

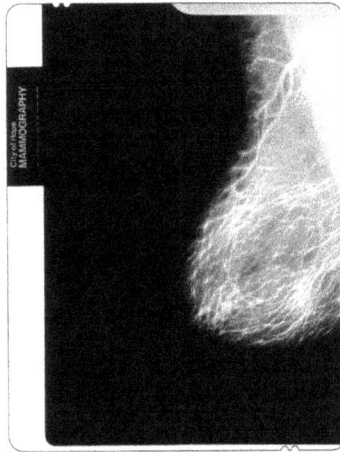

WHY WOMEN GO OUT OF THEIR WAY FOR SOMETHING THEY HATE.

City of Hope

The Power of the True Concept

An image that merely illustrates the headline or a headline that simply explains the visual are both common creative approaches that parade as concepts but are actually just lazy work. A true concept presents a visual that is provocative but does not tell the whole story. The headline makes a bold statement, but is not entirely clear all by itself. Together, they stimulate an explosion of understanding in the mind of the viewer that is more powerful and more memorable than any decorated headline can ever be. That is because the viewer becomes a participant in creating the meaning and is rewarded with a legitimate "aha!" moment that touches on emotion as well as intellect. Viewers are not TOLD the meaning, they EXPERIENCE it.

Be Bold

Don't insist on conventional techniques. What you have been doing, what your competitors are doing, or what you expect may not lead to the best results. Gutsy, genuinely innovative creative work is far more powerful than safe clichés. Safe work is bland work, hence not very effective. Hence not really safe. It dilutes your image, robs you of individuality, and erodes your credibility as a leader. Safe work can kill your brand and your company.

Timely Review — Then Stop Reviewing

The further down the line you get, the more expensive it is to make changes. For that reason, it is important to get your marketing, regulatory, and legal ducks in a row BEFORE you input the agency on a new project. Likewise, the time to request changes to copy is while it is still in manuscript stage—before it becomes part of a design layout. The time to request layout revisions is when it is still in the hand-drawn or computer-generated comp stage and before it becomes a mechanical or printer's proof.

I once worked with very young and inexperienced Product Managers at a large company who would continue to make changes to the copy and the graphic treatment through the blueline stage (printer's proof) on every project. No matter how many times the agency Account Executive tried to tell them that it was a bit late to be making changes, they nonetheless insisted. And, of course, when they got the bill, they always complained that they were being overcharged for the work. That bad habit cost their company many thousands of extra dollars. And it ultimately cost the agency the account when the Product Managers tried to duck responsibility by blaming the agency for the problem. The moral of the story is that when you fail to be disciplined, everybody loses.

Corporate Doublespeak and Other Death Traps

Companies often develop awful slogans and complicated phrases that have absolutely no communication value outside the select group of company collaborators who have fallen in love with their own cleverness. Sometimes a powerful executive—often the CEO—will come up with something (s)he thinks is terribly clever and will force it on everyone else, including the agency. AVOID THAT TRAP.

Think of yourself as a patient with a terminal disease. You would never go to a doctor, diagnose your own condition, and insist that he or she prescribe what you think will cure you. You are not qualified to be your own doctor. Think of your advertising agency as a group of professionals who are trained and experienced in diagnosing your marketing communications condition and prescribing the appropriate remedy. Use that expertise. Don't substitute your own naive word games and visual gimmicks for seasoned expertise. If your agency does not diagnose accurately and prescribe effectively, go to another specialist. But don't jump into the breach with your own in-bred ideas.

It's always possible, of course, that your ideas are very good. Maybe even brilliant. And that's a dilemma. You have to make some decisions. Knowing that there is typically a variety of equally valid creative solutions for any given communications problem, you have to decide whether your idea is so good, such a potential market-killer, that it's worth demoralizing the creative team by insisting on it. If it's just a good idea, but not necessarily the only great solution, then you may humbly present it to the creative team as "something to think about...to get the creative juices flowing." If approached as equal members of the team, the creatives may well treat your ideas with the same respect they accord their own. In that scenario, your ideas may take on a power and grandeur that will surprise you. If you continually treat the creatives with respect, you may even ascend to the exalted rank of honorary member of the creative team.

Think About the Real Customer

In working with the creative team and evaluating creative work, do not use your personal preferences as a yardstick of what is good and bad. You may hate yellow. Or blue. Or red. That does not mean your audience shares your prejudice. You may like one-word headlines. Your audience may like a little more information. Maybe even a clue about what you're trying to tell them. Do research. Do concept and copy testing. Trust the instincts of your agency. If they consistently develop work that does not produce results, get another agency. If they typically develop appropriate marketing strategy and effective creative work, love them, cherish them, reward them, and forgive them the occasional blunder. More often than not, if they present creative that is off-target, they were working with insufficient or inaccurate input.

Years ago, my agency launched a new over-the-counter product with a name the lead venture capital group hated and a graphic style that was exactly the opposite of what they had originally wanted. The product was aimed at women 18-34. The venture capital group consisted of men in their 50's and 60's. Our approach was based on market research. Theirs was based on personal opinion. We prevailed. After only three months on the market, the product broke all records for a new product launch in that category. A year after the launch—after the client went public and the venture capital company had earned many times their initial investment—the President of the lead venture capital group visited the agency to thank us for not allowing them to compromise the brand strategy.

Following personal preferences is a common mistake of young, inexperienced product managers who are being "rotated" through the company on their way to the executive ranks. It is amazing that companies would entrust major brands to people in their early twenties who have limited experience and unproven judgment. It is typical for people in this situation to fly by the seat of their pants (or skirts), following their instincts and using themselves as the litmus test of what customers will respond to. These are usually very smart people. But they are not the customer and may not really understand the psychology of the customer as well as they think they do. Again, do research, do concept testing, do copy testing, and listen to your agency.

Keep it Simple

Avoid complex, restrictive formats and rigid style formulas. Keep things simple. It is extremely important to maintain brand integrity and to create a unique and consistent look, feel, attitude, and personality for your brands. But complex and rigid formats that dictate everything make it virtually impossible to develop powerful creative work. Rules like "The headline will be in helvetica bold small caps in a rectangular box exactly 11/16" from the top edge and 13/16" from the left edge of the ad with a 36% drop shadow at a 7° angle to the right and below the box," are just plain suicide. Rules about the type of photograph or illustration, how they are handled, how they relate to the headline and so forth tend to be arbitrary and typically lead to sterile work. Every concept is (or should be) a unique event in the ongoing corporate dialogue with its constituencies. Each concept should grow out of the marketing message and the type of execution that best

33

communicates that specific message. If they are all the same, your marketing messages will be lost in the overwhelming major message: *This company is boring and phony.*

Be Careful Whose Opinion You Seek

Creative work is best produced by a team composed of a writer and art director and reviewed by the agency Creative Director and Account Executive and the client Marketing Director. Once you start involving other people, the quality of the work goes rapidly downhill. Suzy wants a bigger logo. Bob wants the name of the product in the headline. Tommy wants a snipe announcing the new model. Lorraine really doesn't care for the color of the background. The President thinks the name of the company should be at the top of the ad reversed out of a black box. The Sales Manager once saw an ad run by a competitor that had a photo of the product at an angle in the middle of the ad with a drop shadow, could we do something like that?

It has aptly been said that a camel is a horse designed by a committee. If you subject professional creative work to a panel of amateur judges, it will quickly demoralize your creative team and castrate your marketing program. Use your own judgment and follow the research.

General Guidelines

Good Creative

- It's not "cool"—it's effective
- Achieves specific communications objectives
- Reinforces branding and positioning strategies
- It's not what you like—it's what works

What's The Point?

- Every creative effort should have a specific purpose—a *call to action*
- You want the audience to DO SOMETHING—not always "buy the product"
- You need to tell the audience why they should do what you want them to do—what is the Reason Why they should respond to the Call to Action?

Chapter 6

What Kind of Agency Do You Need?

You have a lot of choices. Today there are virtual agencies, boutique agencies, specialized agencies, regional agencies, and old-line agencies with large staffs of people and offices all over the world. There are also design shops, web design and interactive shops, video producers, event producers, exhibit booth houses, public relations firms from one-person shops to multinational conglomerates, and a long list of other options.

In the old days, a client would call their big advertising agency and say, "I need a trade booth, a speech for the President, a theme for a VIP dinner, some publicity around the event, and some marketing. Let's meet tomorrow and do some planning."

Simple. Turn it over to the agency and let them coordinate all the necessary specialists, get prices, and manage the whole thing. If your company is big enough to afford it, that's still the most efficient way to get it done. However, these days, not every company that needs those kinds of services can afford a large, traditional agency with lots of people on the payroll. So what do you do?

If you have the time, you could hire individual specialists to take on the various tasks under your direction. That would be the cheapest method, but would eat up a lot of internal time, which also costs money.

Another option would be to hire a virtual agency—typically a one- or two-person shop that works with a cadre of external consultants and freelancers—and turn the program over to them. You would get the same coordination and project management as you would get from a big agency, but at considerably lower cost.

A third option would be to do most of the planning and creative work in-house and contract out any production work you could not handle internally. Again, that would require considerable in-house time and effort, but would keep external costs down. However, unless you have a big budget for highly talented and experienced creative people, you are not likely to get the level of quality you would get from an established agency. And, frankly, if you are prepared to invest that kind of money in creative talent, you may come out better selecting a good external agency rather than supporting internal staff. It is likely that a brick-and-mortar, fully staffed traditional agency or a virtual agency would deliver better work for less money.

An important factor to consider is return on investment. Let's say you spend $1 million per year on your marketing budget and "save" $100,000 by doing the work in-house. So you are spending $50,000 on in-house staff instead of $150,000 in agency fees (at the traditional rate of 15%—not always the case). Of course, you are not really saving that money because you are spending all or most of the difference on benefits, facilities, payroll taxes, technology, liability insurance, etc. But let's say you are saving it.

If your marketing program produces a 5% return, you cover the cost of your in-house staff. However, a 5% return is not very good. With great positioning strategy, messaging, and execution, you may be able to get 10%, 15%, 20% or more depending upon your industry and where your product is in its life cycle. Let's say you would get a 15% return on investment with a professional agency. That means you just left $100,000 on the table. Not to mention the increased management time and other ancillary costs associated with having employees.

I have worked with several clients who maintained internal communications staff. If you do a lot of internal communications work (PowerPoint® presentations, flyers, announcements, posters, etc.), it can be extremely efficient and cost-effective compared with outsourcing all of those services. However, for serious marketing communications, there is no internal equivalent for seasoned, professional specialists who work with professional communications agencies.

I leave you with a quote I discovered years ago and have proven over and over again how wise and accurate it is.

Quality doesn't cost, it pays.

About the Author

Stanley Newhoff has been a marketing communications leader for more than thirty years. His experience spans virtually every category, including consumer, business-to-business, medical, technical, and public service. He has worked with some of the biggest and some of the smallest marketing communications companies in the world. He currently heads up Newhoff Healthcare Communications LLC, a marketing communications agency primarily focused on medical marketing and advertising.

As you will note when you read this book, Newhoff pulls no punches. He tells it like it is. As he likes to say, "The truth will set you free."

Feedback is Welcome

Please send comments, corrections, and suggestions for additional topics to be covered in later editions of this book to **feedback@firefishpublishing.com**. And please remember to mention the name of the book. Suggestions for other books are also welcome.

Thank you!

Firefish
PUBLISHING COMPANY

www.ingramcontent.com/pod-product-compliance
Lightning Source LLC
Chambersburg PA
CBHW052111230326
41599CB00055B/5736